COUPLE GOALS

Copyright © 2018 COUPLE GOALS
All rights reserved. This book or any portion thereof
may not be reproduced or used in any manner whatsoever
without the express written permission of the publisher
except for the use of brief quotations in a book review.
Printed Worldwide
First Printing, 2018

COUPLE GOALS

The perfect life does not just happen, it has to be built. This bucket list book is a fun tool for couples to help them achieve their life goals. In this modern age where people are constantly busy, it's easy to let your dreams slip by, and one day you could realise it's too late. This book is designed to help you stop saying "one day we will", or " It would be amazing if we". It's important to narrow down the most important things you would like to achieve together, and then set the date to have them achieved them by. Then do it!

What should I put on my bucket list?

Your bucket list should be unique to you. It does not matter how big or small your couple goals are. You could decide that you would like to do something small like: share picnic in the sun together, or you could decide that you would like to spend a month traveling the world together.

How should we start to fill out our bucket list?

First start at the contents pages, this is a good place to start noting down ideas.

Once you have filled out an idea on the contents pages, find an empty bucket list page, write down the date and the goal, and then note down the page number in the contents page - so you can find it once you have completed the goal.

What to do when a bucket list goal is complete?

First tick off the goal on the contents page, and then find the corresponding bucket list page. Fill out the questions, and then use the notes area to add photos, tickets or write down more about the experience.

Bucket list contents

Page Number	Bucket List Goal	Completion Date	Done ☑

Page Number	Bucket List Goal	Completion Date	Done ✓

Bucket list contents

Bucket list contents

Page Number	Bucket List Goal	Completion Date	Done ☑

Bucket list contents

Page Number	Bucket List Goal	Completion Date	Done ✓

Date ____/____/20____

Bucket list goal: ....

Completed ☐   Date Completed ____/____/20____

Where _____

How was the experience? _____
_____
_____
_____
_____

Notes, Photos, Drawings of the experience

Date ____/____/20____

Bucket list goal: ....

Completed ☐   Date Completed ____/____/20____

Where _____

How was the experience? _____
_____
_____
_____
_____

Notes, Photos, Drawings of the experience

Date ____/____/20____

Bucket list goal: ....

Completed ☐   **Date Completed** ____/____/20____

Where _____

How was the experience? _____
_____
_____
_____
_____

Notes, Photos, Drawings of the experience

Date ____/____/20____

Bucket list goal: ....

Completed ☐   Date Completed ____/____/20____

Where _____

How was the experience? _____
_____
_____
_____
_____

Notes, Photos, Drawings of the experience

Date ____/____/20____

Bucket list goal: ....

Completed ☐   **Date Completed** ____/____/20____

Where _____

How was the experience? _____
_____
_____
_____
_____

Notes, Photos, Drawings of the experience

Date ____/____/20____

Bucket list goal: ....

Completed ☐   Date Completed ____/____/20____

Where _____

How was the experience? _____
_____
_____
_____
_____

Notes, Photos, Drawings of the experience

Date ____/____/20____

Bucket list goal: ....

Completed ☐ **Date Completed** ____/____/20____

Where _____

How was the experience? _____
_____
_____
_____
_____

Notes, Photos, Drawings of the experience

Date ____/____/20____

Bucket list goal: ....

Completed ☐   **Date Completed** ____/____/20____

Where _____

How was the experience? _____
_____
_____
_____
_____

Notes, Photos, Drawings of the experience

Date ____/____/20____

Bucket list goal: ....

Completed ☐   **Date Completed** ____/____/20____

Where _____

How was the experience? _____
_____
_____
_____
_____

Notes, Photos, Drawings of the experience

Date ____/____/20____

Bucket list goal: ....

Completed ☐   Date Completed ____/____/20____

Where _____

How was the experience? _____
_____
_____
_____
_____

Notes, Photos, Drawings of the experience

Date ____/____/20____

Bucket list goal: ....

Completed ☐   **Date Completed** ____/____/20____

Where _____

How was the experience? _____
_____
_____
_____
_____

Notes, Photos, Drawings of the experience

Date ____/____/20____

Bucket list goal: ....

Completed ☐   Date Completed ____/____/20____

Where _____

How was the experience? _____
_____
_____
_____
_____

Notes, Photos, Drawings of the experience

Date ____/____/20____

Bucket list goal: ....

Completed ☐ **Date Completed** ____/____/20____

Where _____

How was the experience? _____
_____
_____
_____
_____

Notes, Photos, Drawings of the experience

Date ____/____/20____

Bucket list goal: ....

Completed ☐   Date Completed ____/____/20____

Where _____

How was the experience? _____
_____
_____
_____
_____

Notes, Photos, Drawings of the experience

Date ____/____/20____

Bucket list goal: ....

Completed ☐   **Date Completed** ____/____/20____

Where _____

How was the experience? _____
_____
_____
_____
_____

Notes, Photos, Drawings of the experience

Date ____/____/20____

Bucket list goal: ....

Completed ☐   Date Completed ____/____/20____

Where _____

How was the experience? _____
_____
_____
_____
_____

Notes, Photos, Drawings of the experience

Date ____/____/20____

Bucket list goal: ....

Completed ☐   Date Completed ____/____/20____

Where _____

How was the experience? _____
_____
_____
_____
_____

Notes, Photos, Drawings of the experience

Date ____/____/20____

Bucket list goal: ....

Completed ☐   Date Completed ____/____/20____

Where _____

How was the experience? _____
_____
_____
_____
_____

Notes, Photos, Drawings of the experience

Date ____/____/20____

Bucket list goal: ....

Completed ☐   **Date Completed** ____/____/20____

Where _____

How was the experience? _____
_____
_____
_____
_____

Notes, Photos, Drawings of the experience

Date ____/____/20____

Bucket list goal: ....

Completed ☐   Date Completed ____/____/20____

Where _____

How was the experience? _____
_____
_____
_____
_____

Notes, Photos, Drawings of the experience

Date ____/____/20____

Bucket list goal: ....

Completed ☐ **Date Completed** ____/____/20____

Where _____

How was the experience? _____
_____
_____
_____
_____

Notes, Photos, Drawings of the experience

Date ____/____/20____

Bucket list goal: ....

Completed ☐   Date Completed ____/____/20____

Where _____

How was the experience? _____
_____
_____
_____
_____

Notes, Photos, Drawings of the experience

Date ____/____/20____

Bucket list goal: ....

Completed ☐   **Date Completed** ____/____/20____

Where _____

How was the experience? _____
_____
_____
_____
_____

Notes, Photos, Drawings of the experience

Date ____/____/20____

Bucket list goal: ....

Completed ☐   Date Completed ____/____/20____

Where _____

How was the experience? _____
_____
_____
_____
_____

Notes, Photos, Drawings of the experience

Date ____/____/20____

Bucket list goal: ....

Completed ☐   **Date Completed** ____/____/20____

Where _____

How was the experience? _____
_____
_____
_____
_____

Notes, Photos, Drawings of the experience

Date ____/____/20____

Bucket list goal: ....

Completed ☐   Date Completed ____/____/20____

Where _____

How was the experience? _____
_____
_____
_____
_____

Notes, Photos, Drawings of the experience

Date ____/____/20____

Bucket list goal: ....

Completed ☐   Date Completed ____/____/20____

Where _____

How was the experience? _____
_____
_____
_____
_____

Notes, Photos, Drawings of the experience

Date ____/____/20____

Bucket list goal: ....

Completed ☐   Date Completed ____/____/20____

Where _____

How was the experience? _____
_____
_____
_____
_____

Notes, Photos, Drawings of the experience

Date ____/____/20____

Bucket list goal: ....

Completed ☐   **Date Completed** ____/____/20____

Where _____

How was the experience? _____
_____
_____
_____
_____

Notes, Photos, Drawings of the experience

Date ____/____/20____

Bucket list goal: ....

Completed ☐   **Date Completed** ____/____/20____

Where _____

How was the experience? _____
_____
_____
_____
_____

Notes, Photos, Drawings of the experience

Date ____/____/20_____

Bucket list goal: ....

Completed ☐   **Date Completed** ____/____/20___

Where _____

How was the experience? _____
_____
_____
_____
_____

Notes, Photos, Drawings of the experience

Date ____/____/20____

Bucket list goal: ....

Completed ☐   Date Completed ____/____/20____

Where _____

How was the experience? _____
_____
_____
_____
_____

Notes, Photos, Drawings of the experience

Date ____/____/20____

Bucket list goal: ....

Completed ☐   Date Completed ____/____/20____

Where _____

How was the experience? _____
_____
_____
_____
_____

Notes, Photos, Drawings of the experience

Date ____/____/20____

Bucket list goal: ....

Completed ☐   Date Completed ____/____/20____

Where _____

How was the experience? _____
_____
_____
_____
_____

Notes, Photos, Drawings of the experience

Date ____/____/20____

Bucket list goal: ....

Completed ☐   **Date Completed** ____/____/20____

Where _____

How was the experience? _____
_____
_____
_____
_____

Notes, Photos, Drawings of the experience

Date ____/____/20____

Bucket list goal: ....

Completed ☐   Date Completed ____/____/20____

Where _____

How was the experience? _____
_____
_____
_____
_____

Notes, Photos, Drawings of the experience

Date ____/____/20____

Bucket list goal: ....

Completed ☐   **Date Completed** ____/____/20____

Where _____

How was the experience? _____
_____
_____
_____
_____

Notes, Photos, Drawings of the experience

Date ___/___/20___

Bucket list goal: ....

Completed ☐   Date Completed ___/___/20___

Where _____

How was the experience? _____
_____
_____
_____
_____

Notes, Photos, Drawings of the experience

Date ____/____/20____

Bucket list goal: ....

Completed ☐   **Date Completed** ___/___/20___

Where _____

How was the experience? _____
_____
_____
_____
_____

Notes, Photos, Drawings of the experience

Date ___/___/20___

Bucket list goal: ....

Completed ☐ Date Completed ___/___/20___

Where _____

How was the experience? _____
_____
_____
_____
_____

Notes, Photos, Drawings of the experience

Date ____/____/20____

Bucket list goal: ....

Completed ☐   Date Completed ____/____/20____

Where _____

How was the experience? _____
_____
_____
_____
_____

Notes, Photos, Drawings of the experience

Date ____/____/20____

Bucket list goal: ....

Completed ☐   Date Completed ____/____/20____

Where _____

How was the experience? _____
_____
_____
_____
_____

Notes, Photos, Drawings of the experience

Date ____/____/20____

Bucket list goal: ....

Completed ☐   **Date Completed** ____/____/20____

Where _____

How was the experience? _____
_____
_____
_____
_____

Notes, Photos, Drawings of the experience

Date ____/____/20____

Bucket list goal: ....

Completed ☐   Date Completed ____/____/20____

Where _____

How was the experience? _____
_____
_____
_____
_____

Notes, Photos, Drawings of the experience

Date ____/____/20____

Bucket list goal: ....

Completed ☐　　**Date Completed** ____/____/20____

Where _____

How was the experience? _____
_____
_____
_____
_____

Notes, Photos, Drawings of the experience

Date ____/____/20____

Bucket list goal: ....

Completed ☐   Date Completed ____/____/20____

Where _____

How was the experience? _____
_____
_____
_____
_____

Notes, Photos, Drawings of the experience

Date ____/____/20____

Bucket list goal: ....

Completed ☐   **Date Completed** ____/____/20____

Where _____

How was the experience? _____
_____
_____
_____
_____

Notes, Photos, Drawings of the experience

Date ___/___/20___

Bucket list goal: ....

Completed ☐   Date Completed ___/___/20___

Where _____

How was the experience? _____
_____
_____
_____
_____

Notes, Photos, Drawings of the experience

Date ____/____/20____

Bucket list goal: ....

Completed ☐ **Date Completed** ____/____/20____

Where _____

How was the experience? _____
_____
_____
_____
_____

Notes, Photos, Drawings of the experience

Date ___/___/20___

Bucket list goal: ....

Completed ☐   Date Completed ___/___/20___

Where _____

How was the experience? _____
_____
_____
_____
_____

Notes, Photos, Drawings of the experience

Date ____/____/20____

Bucket list goal: ....

Completed ☐ **Date Completed** ____/____/20____

Where _____

How was the experience? _____
_____
_____
_____
_____

Notes, Photos, Drawings of the experience

Date ___/___/20___

Bucket list goal: ....

Completed ☐ Date Completed ___/___/20___

Where _____

How was the experience? _____
_____
_____
_____
_____

Notes, Photos, Drawings of the experience

Date ____/____/20_____

Bucket list goal: ....

Completed ☐   **Date Completed** ____/____/20____

Where _____

How was the experience? _____
_____
_____
_____
_____

Notes, Photos, Drawings of the experience

Date ___/___/20___

Bucket list goal: ....

Completed ☐   Date Completed ___/___/20___

Where _____

How was the experience? _____
_____
_____
_____
_____

Notes, Photos, Drawings of the experience

Date ___/___/20___

Bucket list goal: ....

Completed ☐   **Date Completed** ___/___/20___

Where _____

How was the experience? _____
_____
_____
_____
_____

Notes, Photos, Drawings of the experience

Date ____/____/20____

Bucket list goal: ....

Completed ☐   Date Completed ____/____/20____

Where _____

How was the experience? _____
_____
_____
_____
_____

Notes, Photos, Drawings of the experience

Date ____/____/20____

Bucket list goal: ....

Completed ☐   Date Completed ____/____/20____

Where _____

How was the experience? _____
_____
_____
_____
_____

Notes, Photos, Drawings of the experience

Date ___/___/20___

Bucket list goal: ....

Completed ☐   Date Completed ___/___/20___

Where _____

How was the experience? _____
_____
_____
_____
_____

Notes, Photos, Drawings of the experience

Date ____/____/20____

Bucket list goal: ....

Completed ☐   **Date Completed** ____/____/20____

Where _____

How was the experience? _____
_____
_____
_____
_____

Notes, Photos, Drawings of the experience

Date ____/____/20____

Bucket list goal: ....

Completed ☐   Date Completed ____/____/20____

Where _____

How was the experience? _____
_____
_____
_____
_____

Notes, Photos, Drawings of the experience

Date ____/____/20____

Bucket list goal: ....

Completed ☐   **Date Completed** ____/____/20____

Where _____

How was the experience? _____
_____
_____
_____
_____

Notes, Photos, Drawings of the experience

Date ____/____/20____

Bucket list goal: ....

Completed ☐   Date Completed ____/____/20____

Where _____

How was the experience? _____
_____
_____
_____
_____

Notes, Photos, Drawings of the experience

Date ____/____/20____

Bucket list goal: ....

Completed ☐ **Date Completed** ____/____/20____

Where _____

How was the experience? _____
_____
_____
_____
_____

Notes, Photos, Drawings of the experience

Date ___/___/20___

Bucket list goal: ....

Completed ☐   Date Completed ___/___/20___

Where _____

How was the experience? _____
_____
_____
_____
_____

Notes, Photos, Drawings of the experience

Date ____/____/20____

Bucket list goal: ....

Completed ☐ **Date Completed** ____/____/20____

Where _____

How was the experience? _____
_____
_____
_____
_____

Notes, Photos, Drawings of the experience

Date ___/___/20___

Bucket list goal: ....

Completed ☐   Date Completed ___/___/20___

Where _____

How was the experience? _____
_____
_____
_____
_____

Notes, Photos, Drawings of the experience

Date ____/____/20____

Bucket list goal: ....

Completed ☐   Date Completed ____/____/20____

Where _____

How was the experience? _____
_____
_____
_____
_____

Notes, Photos, Drawings of the experience

Date ____/____/20____

Bucket list goal: ....

Completed ☐   Date Completed ____/____/20____

Where _____

How was the experience? _____
_____
_____
_____
_____

Notes, Photos, Drawings of the experience

Date ____/____/20____

Bucket list goal: ....

Completed ☐   **Date Completed** ____/____/20____

Where _____

How was the experience? _____
_____
_____
_____
_____

Notes, Photos, Drawings of the experience

Date ___/___/20___

Bucket list goal: ....

Completed ☐   **Date Completed** ___/___/20___

Where _____

How was the experience? _____
_____
_____
_____
_____

Notes, Photos, Drawings of the experience

Date ____/____/20____

Bucket list goal: ....

Completed ☐   **Date Completed** ____/____/20____

Where _____

How was the experience? _____
_____
_____
_____
_____

Notes, Photos, Drawings of the experience

Date ____/____/20____

Bucket list goal: ....

Completed ☐   Date Completed ____/____/20____

Where _____

How was the experience? _____
_____
_____
_____
_____

Notes, Photos, Drawings of the experience

Date ____/____/20____

Bucket list goal: ....

Completed ☐   **Date Completed** ____/____/20____

Where _____

How was the experience? _____
_____
_____
_____
_____

Notes, Photos, Drawings of the experience

Date ____/____/20____

Bucket list goal: ....

Completed ☐   Date Completed ____/____/20____

Where _____

How was the experience? _____
_____
_____
_____
_____

Notes, Photos, Drawings of the experience

Date ____/____/20____

Bucket list goal: ....

Completed ☐   **Date Completed** ____/____/20____

Where _____

How was the experience? _____
_____
_____
_____
_____

Notes, Photos, Drawings of the experience

Date ____/____/20____

Bucket list goal: ....

Completed ☐   Date Completed ____/____/20____

Where _____

How was the experience? _____
_____
_____
_____
_____

Notes, Photos, Drawings of the experience

Date ____/____/20____

Bucket list goal: ....

Completed ☐   **Date Completed** ____/____/20____

Where _____

How was the experience? _____
_____
_____
_____
_____

Notes, Photos, Drawings of the experience

Date ___/___/20___

Bucket list goal: ....

Completed ☐   Date Completed ___/___/20___

Where _____

How was the experience? _____
_____
_____
_____
_____

Notes, Photos, Drawings of the experience

Date ____/____/20____

Bucket list goal: ....

Completed ☐   **Date Completed** ____/____/20____

Where _____

How was the experience? _____
_____
_____
_____
_____

Notes, Photos, Drawings of the experience

Date ____/____/20____

Bucket list goal: ....

Completed ☐   Date Completed ____/____/20____

Where _____

How was the experience? _____
_____
_____
_____
_____

Notes, Photos, Drawings of the experience

Date ____/____/20____

Bucket list goal: ....

Completed ☐   Date Completed ____/____/20____

Where _____

How was the experience? _____
_____
_____
_____
_____

Notes, Photos, Drawings of the experience

Date ___/___/20___

Bucket list goal: ....

Completed ☐   Date Completed ___/___/20___

Where _____

How was the experience? _____
_____
_____
_____
_____

Notes, Photos, Drawings of the experience

Date ____/____/20____

Bucket list goal: ....

Completed ☐   **Date Completed** ____/____/20____

Where _____

How was the experience? _____

Notes, Photos, Drawings of the experience

Date ____/____/20____

Bucket list goal: ....

Completed ☐ **Date Completed** ____/____/20____

Where _____

How was the experience? _____
_____
_____
_____
_____

Notes, Photos, Drawings of the experience

Date ____/____/20____

Bucket list goal: ....

Completed ☐   Date Completed ____/____/20____

Where _____

How was the experience? _____
_____
_____
_____
_____

Notes, Photos, Drawings of the experience

Date ___/___/20___

Bucket list goal: ....

Completed ☐   Date Completed ___/___/20___

Where _____

How was the experience? _____
_____
_____
_____
_____

Notes, Photos, Drawings of the experience

Date ____/____/20____

Bucket list goal: ....

Completed ☐   Date Completed ____/____/20____

Where _____

How was the experience? _____
_____
_____
_____
_____

Notes, Photos, Drawings of the experience

Date ____/____/20____

Bucket list goal: ....

Completed ☐   Date Completed ____/____/20____

Where _____

How was the experience? _____
_____
_____
_____
_____

Notes, Photos, Drawings of the experience

Date ____/____/20____

Bucket list goal: ....

Completed ☐   **Date Completed** ____/____/20____

Where _____

How was the experience? _____
_____
_____
_____
_____

Notes, Photos, Drawings of the experience

Date ____/____/20____

Bucket list goal: ....

Completed ☐   Date Completed ____/____/20____

Where _____

How was the experience? _____
_____
_____
_____
_____

Notes, Photos, Drawings of the experience

Date ____/____/20____

Bucket list goal: ....

Completed ☐   Date Completed ____/____/20____

Where _____

How was the experience? _____
_____
_____
_____
_____

Notes, Photos, Drawings of the experience

Date ____/____/20____

Bucket list goal: ....

Completed ☐   Date Completed ____/____/20____

Where _____

How was the experience? _____
_____
_____
_____
_____

Notes, Photos, Drawings of the experience

Date ____/____/20____

Bucket list goal: ....

Completed ☐   **Date Completed** ____/____/20____

Where _____

How was the experience? _____
_____
_____
_____
_____

Notes, Photos, Drawings of the experience

Date ____/____/20____

Bucket list goal: ....

Completed ☐   Date Completed ____/____/20____

Where _____

How was the experience? _____
_____
_____
_____
_____

Notes, Photos, Drawings of the experience

Date ____/____/20____

Bucket list goal: ....

Completed ☐   **Date Completed** ____/____/20____

Where _____

How was the experience? _____
_____
_____
_____
_____

Notes, Photos, Drawings of the experience

Date ____/____/20____

Bucket list goal: ....

Completed ☐   Date Completed ____/____/20____

Where _____

How was the experience? _____
_____
_____
_____
_____

Notes, Photos, Drawings of the experience

Date ____/____/20____

Bucket list goal: ....

Completed ☐ Date Completed ____/____/20____

Where _____

How was the experience? _____
_____
_____
_____
_____

Notes, Photos, Drawings of the experience

Date ____/____/20____

Bucket list goal: ....

Completed ☐   Date Completed ____/____/20____

Where _____

How was the experience? _____

_____
_____
_____
_____

Notes, Photos, Drawings of the experience

Date ____/____/20____

Bucket list goal: ....

Completed ☐   **Date Completed** ____/____/20____

Where _____

How was the experience? _____
_____
_____
_____
_____

Notes, Photos, Drawings of the experience

Date ____/____/20____

Bucket list goal: ....

Completed ☐   Date Completed ____/____/20____

Where _____

How was the experience? _____
_____
_____
_____
_____

Notes, Photos, Drawings of the experience

Date ____/____/20____

Bucket list goal: ....

Completed ☐   **Date Completed** ____/____/20____

Where _____

How was the experience? _____
_____
_____
_____
_____

Notes, Photos, Drawings of the experience

Date ____/____/20____

Bucket list goal: ....

Completed ☐   **Date Completed** ____/____/20____

Where _____

How was the experience? _____
_____
_____
_____
_____

Notes, Photos, Drawings of the experience

Date ____/____/20____

Bucket list goal: ....

Completed ☐   Date Completed ____/____/20____

Where _____

How was the experience? _____
_____
_____
_____
_____

Notes, Photos, Drawings of the experience

Date ___/___/20___

Bucket list goal: ....

Completed ☐   Date Completed ___/___/20___

Where _____

How was the experience? _____
_____
_____
_____
_____

Notes, Photos, Drawings of the experience

Date ____/____/20____

Bucket list goal: ....

Completed ☐   **Date Completed** ____/____/20____

Where _____

How was the experience? _____
_____
_____
_____
_____

Notes, Photos, Drawings of the experience

Made in the USA
Middletown, DE
11 February 2020